America at WAR

Civil WAR

TEN GREATEST HEROES

John Perritano

Created by Q2AMedia
www.q2amedia.com

Text, design & illustrations Copyright © Q2AMedia 2011

Editor Jessica Cohn
Project Manager Shekhar Kapur
Art Director Joita Das
Designers Deepika Verma, Isha Khanna and Ritu Chopra
Picture Researchers Akansha Srivastava and Nivisha Sinha

10 9 8 7 6 5 4 3 2 1

ISBN10: 93-810870-0-8
ISBN13: 978-9-381-08700-8

Printed in China

Picture Credits
t=top, b=bottom, l=left, r=right, c=center, tl=top left, tc=top center, tr=top right, bl=bottom left, br=bottom right, tb=top bottom

Cover Page: Mort Kunstler, Inc.
Back Cover: The Print Collector/Photolibrary.
Title Page: DoDmedia.
Imprint Page: Library of Congress.

4t Library of Congress. 4b Currier & Ives: Library of Congress. 5t Library of Congress. 6t Library of Congress. 6-7 Sidney E. King: National Park Service. 7t Library of Congress. 8 Library of Congress. 9 Library of Congress. 10 Hulton Archive: Getty Images. 11 Ogden,

Henry Alexander: Library of Congress. 12t Library of Congress. 12-13 Kurz & Allison: Library of Congress. 14 Library of Congress. 15t Library of Congress. 15c Andrew J. Russell: AP Photo. 15 Ken Welsh: Photolibrary. 16t Library of Congress. 16-17 Library of Congress. 18t Library of Congress. 18b North Wind Picture Archives. 19 North Wind Picture Archives. 20 Library of Congress. 21t Fort Wagner Stormed by the 54th Massachusetts (Colored) Regiment, 18th July 1863 (color litho), American School, (19th century)/Private Collection/Peter Newark American Pictures/The Bridgeman Art Library. 21b Library of Congress. 22t Library of Congress. 22c AP Photo. 23t Library of Congress. 23b Library of Congress. 24 E.G. Middleton & Co: Library of Congress.

24-25 DoDmedia. 26t Magnus Manske. 26c Library of Congress. 26b North Wind Picture Archives. 27 Library of Congress, Portrait of General Jubal A. Early (litho), American School, (19th century)/Private Collection/Peter Newark Military Pictures/The Bridgeman Art Library, Portrait of Lewis A. Armistead (litho), American School, (19th century)/Private Collection/Peter Newark Military Pictures/The Bridgeman Art Library, Library of Congress. 28b DoDmedia. 28t Library of Congress. 29t Library of Congress. 29b Library of Congress. 30 North Wind Picture Archives. 31t Library of Congress. 31b Library of Congress.

Q2AMedia Art Bank: 5, 17, 25.

Contents

A Torn Nation

On April 12, 1861, the citizens of Charleston, South Carolina, hooted and hollered as Confederate General P.T. Beauregard gave the order to fire on Fort Sumter. With those first shots, the Civil War began.

The nation had torn apart. The North and South disagreed on major issues, including slavery and the difference between state and federal rights. Seven Southern states had **seceded** from the Union. Others threatened to follow. The rebellious states had formed the Confederate States of America, also known as the Confederacy.

In January 1861, Southern forces had shot at a supply ship headed to Fort Sumter, a U.S. military stronghold in the Charleston harbor. President Abraham Lincoln had entered office in March. He had sent word to the Southern leadership in early April that U.S. forces would re-supply the U.S. fort.

Renouncing the Confederacy, President Abraham Lincoln said that the U.S. Constitution did not allow the states' separation, and that the wishes of the majority of the Union's people should be honored.

Fort Sumter was on an island in Charleston's harbor. Some of the city's finest families went to the waterfront to watch its bombardment.

Roots of Rebellion

At the time, the nation was expanding westward. Most Northern states had outlawed slavery, and Lincoln did not want slavery to expand into new U.S. **territories**. Leaders in the South believed that slavery was vital to their economy. For decades, the two sides had tried to reach a **compromise** over the issue. Nothing had worked. It seemed that war, not politics, would finally settle the question.

When the war finally ended four years later in April 1865, the Union had decimated the South. By the war's end, the slaves had been freed. However, more than 600,000 Americans had died during the conflict. It was the bloodiest war in U.S. history. Combat was horrific. Those who fought were changed forever. Here are some of their heroic stories.

When the war broke out, about 4 million slaves were working on Southern farms and plantations.

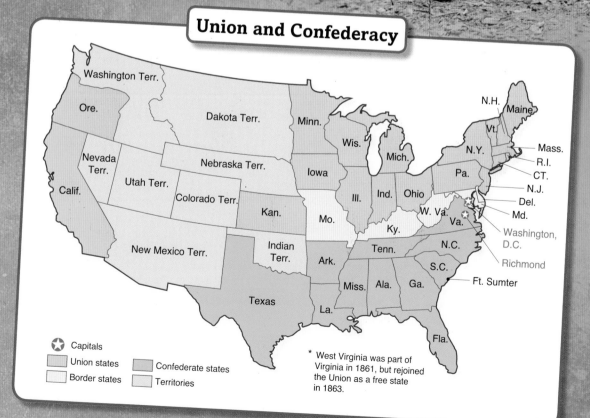

Union and Confederacy

Washington Terr.

Ore.

Dakota Terr.

Minn.

N.H.

Maine

Vt.

Nevada Terr.

Nebraska Terr.

Wis.

Mich.

N.Y.

Mass.

R.I.

Utah Terr.

Iowa

Pa.

CT.

Calif.

Colorado Terr.

Ill.   Ind.   Ohio

N.J.

Del.

Kan.

Mo.

W. Va.

Va.

Md.

Ky.

Washington, D.C.

New Mexico Terr.

Indian Terr.

Ark.

Tenn.

N.C.

Richmond

S.C.

Ft. Sumter

Texas

Miss.   Ala.   Ga.

La.

Fla.

★ Capitals
Union states
Border states
Confederate states
Territories

* West Virginia was part of Virginia in 1861, but rejoined the Union as a free state in 1863.

Thomas "Stonewall" Jackson

"You may be whatever you resolve to be."—*Stonewall Jackson*

Thomas Jackson was no stranger to heartache. His parents died when he was young. Most of his siblings passed away early. He was raised by relatives and given little formal schooling.

A Soldier's Life

At age 18, Jackson entered the U.S. Military Academy at West Point. After graduating, he fought in the Mexican–American War (1846–1848). West Point and the war trained him for the Civil War. He learned many lessons, including how to **outflank** the enemy.

Thomas "Stonewall" Jackson

Born:	January 21, 1824
Hometown:	Clarksburg, Virginia
Loyalties:	Confederacy
Rank:	Lieutenant General
Heroic Moment:	First Battle of Bull Run, also known as First Manassas (July 21, 1861)

Bull Run

When the Civil War began, Jackson sided with Virginia and the newly formed Confederate States of America. He participated in the war's first major land battle on July 21, 1861, when Confederate General P. T. Beauregard faced off against Union General Irvin McDowell at Manassas, Virginia.

McDowell's **objective** was to capture a rail line that ran to Richmond, Virginia, the capital of the Confederacy. His forces outnumbered Beauregard's. But McDowell's troops were undisciplined and had never been in battle. Beauregard was determined to stop the Union advance. He placed his troops along the bank of a creek named Bull Run.

When the fighting began in the morning, McDowell attacked the Confederate left **flank** on Matthews Hill. The Union troops pushed the Confederates to Henry Hill. In the afternoon, however, additional Rebels arrived. Jackson and his Virginia brigade joined the battle. He positioned his men and artillery near Henry Hill House, a key point on the battlefield.

General Irvin McDowell's troops were so undisciplined, they picked berries and left equipment on the roadside during their mission.

"Stonewall"

A Confederate **brigade** commanded by General Bernard E. Bee could see Jackson stand his ground to halt the Union advance. As bullets whizzed past Jackson, Bee shouted to his troops: "There stands Jackson like a stone wall! Rally behind the Virginians!" The Confederate lines held. By mid-afternoon, the Rebels had regrouped and **counterattacked**, overrunning the Union lines. Jackson's steadfastness earned him the nickname "Stonewall."

The defeated Federals fled back to Washington. Before the battle, many Northerners believed the war would end quickly with a Northern victory. Afterward, everyone realized that the Civil War would be a long, deadly conflict.

At the First Battle of Bull Run, both generals planned to attack the right flank of the enemy as a diversion and attack with full strength on the left. But the plans were not executed correctly.

John Singleton Mosby

As the Army of the Potomac slowly slogged toward Richmond, John Singleton Mosby volunteered to serve as a scout for the Confederates. It was a decision that made Mosby a legend.

McClellan and Stuart

Union General George B. McClellan whipped the Army of the Potomac into shape, but he still was not eager to fight. Though his army vastly outnumbered the nearest Confederate force, McClellan remained in Washington.

"If General McClellan does not want to use the army," President Abraham Lincoln said ruefully, "I would like to borrow it for a time." Finally, after much prodding, McClellan marched out of Washington on March 17, 1862. His plan was to ferry Union troops down the Potomac River to the York–James Peninsula in Virginia. Then the Federals would fight their way to Richmond.

Confederate General Robert E. Lee took command of the Rebels. He asked General J.E.B. Stuart to locate the Federals. The Confederate **cavalry** rode north from Richmond on June 12, then turned east across the Chickahominy River. Mosby, their scout, soon returned with exciting news: he had found McClellan's army.

John Singleton Mosby

Born:	December 6, 1833
Hometown:	Powhatan County, Virginia
Loyalties:	Confederacy
Rank:	First Lieutenant
Heroic Moment:	Peninsula Campaign (April–June 1862)

"I fought for success and not for display."—*John Singleton Mosby*

President Abraham Lincoln met with General George B. McClellan in 1862. Lincoln became disenchanted with him as the war wore on.

Wreaking Havoc

Stuart and Mosby came up with a plan. Instead of galloping back to Richmond, the Rebel cavalry would ride around the Army of the Potomac and wreak havoc behind enemy lines. For several days, the Rebel cavalry made daring raids. They captured many enemy soldiers and hundreds of horses and mules. They destroyed tons of Union supplies.

"Greatest Feat of the War"

"I returned yesterday with General Stuart from the grandest scout of the war," Mosby wrote to his wife. "I not only helped to execute it, but was the first one who conceived and demonstrated that it was practicable. Everybody says it was the greatest feat of the war."

Thanks to Mosby, the Confederates drove McClellan's army away from Richmond. The Peninsula Campaign, as it was called, revealed McClellan's weakness as a commander. Lee decided to take advantage of that weakness by invading the North.

J.E.B. Stuart

No one in the Confederate Army seemed as daring or as bold as James Ewell Brown Stuart, known as Jeb. To the South, Stuart was a hero. For those in the North, Stuart was a menace. He fought in most major campaigns of the war.

A Born Leader

Stuart was a born leader. Known for being cheerful, he wore a scarlet-lined cape, a rose in his lapel, and an upturned hat with a feather plume. His ride around McClellan during the Peninsula Campaign made headlines in the North and South. "The whole country is astonished and applauds," *The Richmond Daily Dispatch* said. "McClellan is disgraced." Stuart soon emerged as Lee's top cavalry officer.

J.E.B. Stuart

Born:	February 6, 1833
Hometown:	Patrick County Virginia
Loyalties:	Confederacy
Rank:	Major General
Heroic Moment:	Second Ride around McClellan (October 1862)

"Believe that you can whip the enemy, and you have won half the battle."—*J.E.B. Stuart*

Northern Raid

In September 1862, the Army of Northern Virginia invaded the North for the first time. They suffered a major setback at Antietam Creek, Maryland. Lee's defeated army returned home to Virginia. At the same time, Stuart began a second bold ride around McClellan's army.

Stuart raided the Northern town of Chambersburg, Pennsylvania, located not far from Antietam. His troops looted a Federal **arsenal**. They took guns and clothes, including coats, socks, and underwear. What they couldn't carry, they burned.

The Union cavalry tried to capture Stuart, but they were no match for him. He rode into Cashtown, Pennsylvania, and crossed the Potomac River into Maryland. In Emmitsburg, some of the villagers cheered as Stuart entered their town. He captured more than a thousand horses and several prisoners in the three-day raid.

"Who Is Stuart?"

Stuart's "Second Ride around McClellan" boosted Confederate morale and further damaged McClellan's reputation. McClellan was soon pulled from duty. "Anything more daring, more gallant, and more successful than the foray of General Stuart ... over the border of Maryland and Pennsylvania, has never been recorded," the London *Times* said. Newspapers in New York asked, "Who is Stuart?"

J.E.B. Stuart was a brigadier general when he made the first of his celebrated raids. He was promoted to major general in July 1862.

James Longstreet

Robert E. Lee, leader of the Southern forces, relied on Lieutenant General James Longstreet at crucial times. Fredericksburg was one of them.

Across the Rappahannock

General George McClellan read his new orders from Washington. With a slight smile that hid disappointment, he turned to his visitor and said: "Well, Burnside, I turn the command over to you." McClellan was out of a job—his fate sealed when he failed to destroy Lee's army at Antietam. Union General Ambrose Burnside was now in charge. Burnside quickly marched toward Fredericksburg, Virginia, on the Rappahannock River between Richmond and Washington.

Burnside hoped to capture the hills overlooking the town before Lee had a chance to react. However, Burnside needed **pontoon** bridges to get his army across the Rappahannock. It took 17 days for the bridges to arrive. This left Lee enough time to place his army above the town. Lee asked Longstreet, the man he called his "Old War Horse," to defend several of those hills.

"Why do men fight who are born to be brothers?"—*James Longstreet*

James Longstreet

Born:	January 8, 1821
Hometown:	Edgefield District, South Carolina
Loyalties:	Confederacy
Rank:	Lieutenant General
Heroic Moment:	Fredericksburg (December 11–15, 1862)

Lee's Worries

As Burnside readied for battle, Lee grew worried. He believed Longstreet was in trouble because of the great number of Union troops that had gathered. However, Longstreet was a brilliant **tactician**. When the Union troops arrived at Fredericksburg, Longstreet was ready for them.

At the Battle of Fredericksburg, James Longstreet's troops played a pivotal role in fighting back the Union forces.

Southern Victory

On December 13, Burnside attacked Marye's Heights, a low ridge above Fredericksburg. To reach the hill, the Union soldiers had to march into a valley and then crawl up a slope. Longstreet ordered his well-placed artillery to blast the Federals to pieces.

In just one hour, approximately 3,000 Union troops died, but Burnside kept sending troops. The Federals attacked multiple times. Lee and Longstreet could not believe the carnage. "It is well that war is so terrible. We should grow too fond of it," Lee told Longstreet. Burnside finally retreated. The victory cemented Longstreet's reputation as a great battlefield general.

Robert E. Lee

When Abraham Lincoln became president, he asked Lee to command the Union Army. Lee declined, saying he was duty-bound to fight for Virginia, his home state. Lee soon emerged as one of the most masterful generals of the war. By January 1863, Lincoln was trying to find a commander who could defeat Lee.

Hooker's Plans

That month, Lincoln replaced General Ambrose Burnside with General Joseph B. Hooker. Hooker planned to destroy Lee's army and take Richmond. He sent part of his troops to march against Lee at Fredericksburg, which would force Lee to defend the town. Hooker led the others across the Rappahannock River to attack the Confederates from the rear. "My plans are perfect," Hooker boasted. "May God have mercy on General Lee, for I will have none."

Chancellorsville

Seeing through Hooker's plan, Lee left 10,000 soldiers to defend Fredericksburg. He sent the rest of his command to attack the Union soldiers who had been sent to surprise them. Hooker set up his headquarters in Chancellorsville, west of Fredericksburg, where the main battle erupted.

"Do your duty in all things. You cannot do more; you should never wish to do less."
—*Robert E. Lee*

Robert E. Lee

Date of Birth:	January 19, 1807
Hometown:	Stratford, Virginia
Loyalties:	Confederacy
Rank:	General-in-Chief
Heroic Moment:	Chancellorsville (April 30–May 6, 1863)

The Wilderness

On May 1, Lee and Hooker fought in a heavily wooded area known as the "Wilderness." The brief battle rattled Hooker. He ordered his men to withdraw to a defensive position. Lee quickly went on the offensive. Confederate General Stonewall Jackson led approximately 27,000 men on an attack at the Union's camp the next day. As the Rebels charged, the discouraged Union soldiers retreated.

Union General Joseph B. Hooker fought with distinction throughout the war, but he is often remembered for his defeat at Chancellorsville.

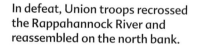

In defeat, Union troops recrossed the Rappahannock River and reassembled on the north bank.

Lee Wins

On May 2, Jackson was wounded accidentally by one of his own soldiers. General J. E. B. Stuart took charge of the Confederates. Stuart launched a dawn attack and drove the Federals out of Chancellorsville. Though a Union force moved on Fredericksburg, Lee masterfully turned his troops and pushed the Federals back. Chancellorsville was Lee's greatest victory. Yet Lee let the Army of the Potomac escape, which would prove to be a grave mistake.

Hooker formed a U-shaped troop formation to defend against the South.

Winfield Scott Hancock

General Winfield Scott Hancock was one of the Union's most physically imposing heroes. His finest moment came during the first day of battle at Gettysburg.

Into the North

Coming off his victory at Chancellorsville, Robert E. Lee decided to once again invade the North. Lee hoped an invasion would turn the people in the North against the war and force Lincoln to seek peace.

On July 1, 1863, Lee's forces advanced through southern Pennsylvania. Two brigades of Union cavalry commanded by Brigadier General John Buford were already in Gettysburg. Buford knew that Gettysburg and the roads around it were strategically important.

About three miles west of town, Buford's troopers spotted the Rebels. Buford's men opened fire. The Rebels swept forward. The Union lines collapsed as the Federals retreated through town.

"My politics are of a practical kind—the integrity of the country, the supremacy of the Federal government, an honorable peace, or none at all."—*Winfield Scott Hancock*

The Battle of Gettysburg began as a skirmish but ended with tens of thousands of dead, wounded, and missing soldiers on both sides.

Winfield Scott Hancock

Date of Birth:	February 14, 1824
Hometown:	Montgomery Square, Pennsylvania
Loyalties:	Union
Rank:	Major General
Heroic Moment:	Gettysburg (July 1–3, 1863)

The Fishhook

Union Major General Winfield Scott Hancock arrived on the chaotic scene. "This battle is the turning point of the war," he said to his troops. "If we win this fight, the war is practically over." Hancock ordered his soldiers to take up positions on the hills. This gave the Union an advantage. The Federal line of defense was shaped like a giant fishhook. The curve of the hook ran along Culp's Hill. The shank crossed Cemetery Ridge. At the end were two hills called Big Round Top and Little Round Top.

Lee's Fate Sealed

Lee ordered Confederate General Richard Ewell to take Culp's Hill and Cemetery Hill before nightfall. Had he quickly obeyed, Ewell might have dislodged the Federals from their positions and given Lee the advantage. However, Ewell waited. Hancock's decision to fortify the high ground sealed Lee's fate at Gettysburg and ultimately doomed the Confederate invasion.

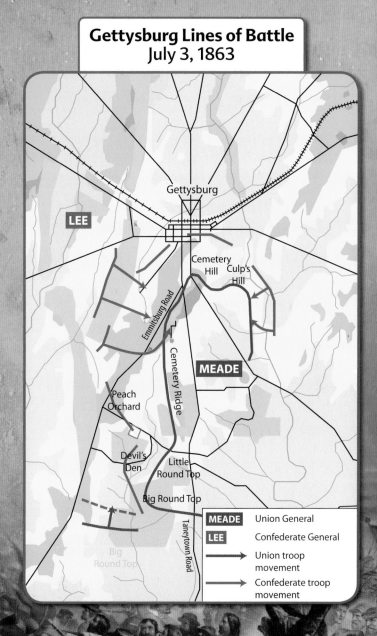

Gettysburg Lines of Battle
July 3, 1863

Gettysburg

LEE

Cemetery Hill

Culp's Hill

Emmitsburg Road

Cemetery Ridge

MEADE

Peach Orchard

Devil's Den

Little Round Top

Big Round Top

Taneytown Road

Big Round Top

MEADE	Union General
LEE	Confederate General
→	Union troop movement
→	Confederate troop movement

17

Joshua Lawrence Chamberlain

Joshua Lawrence Chamberlain did not look like a hero. He had been a bookish college professor in Maine. But on the second day of battle at Gettysburg, Chamberlain became one of the war's greatest heroes.

Day Two at Gettysburg

As the sun came up on July 2, the size of both armies at Gettysburg had grown. Sixty-five thousand Confederates faced 85,000 Federals. Lee wanted to capture Little Round Top, train his cannons on the Federal line on Cemetery Ridge, and smash the Union line to pieces.

"In great deeds something abides. On great fields something stays."
—*Joshua Lawrence Chamberlain*

Joshua Lawrence Chamberlain

Date of Birth:	September 8, 1828
Hometown:	Brewer, Maine
Loyalties:	Union
Rank:	Colonel
Heroic Moment:	Gettysburg (July 1–3, 1863)

A fence along Emmitsburg Road slowed the Confederate advance and allowed the Union to fire directly at them.

High Ground

Lee ordered General James Longstreet to attack the ridge. General George Meade, commander of the Union forces at Gettysburg, ordered General Dan Sickles to protect it. But Sickles disobeyed Meade and moved his men away from Cemetery Ridge. That left Big Round Top and Little Round Top exposed to enemy attack. Before Meade could see the danger, it was too late. Longstreet's men charged. Union General Gouverneur K. Warren quickly sent for **reinforcements**.

The Confederates scrambled up Big Round Top, a move that gave Confederate Colonel William C. Oates a clear view of the battlefield. The Union soldiers had not yet positioned themselves on Little Round Top. But Joshua Chamberlain and other Union soldiers, including a regiment from the 20th Maine, were hustling to plug the hole on the hill.

Charge Down the Hill

Led by Oates, the Confederates made several charges up Little Round Top, driving the Union men from their positions. Each time, the 20th Maine fought its way back. Chamberlain's superiors ordered him to fight to the last man. Ammunition was running low, so Chamberlain desperately ordered his men to fix **bayonets** and charge in defense of Little Round Top. The Union counterattack surprised the Confederates, and they retreated.

Back to Virginia

Chamberlain received the **Congressional Medal of Honor** for his heroics. He and his men prevented Lee from destroying the Union defenses on Cemetery Ridge. The following day, Lee lost the Battle of Gettysburg and retreated to Virginia. The South never invaded the North again.

Robert Gould Shaw

Massachusetts Governor John Andrew asked Colonel Robert Gould Shaw to organize and command the North's first black regiment, the 54th Massachusetts Volunteer Infantry Regiment.

"No Power on Earth"

On January 1, 1863, the Emancipation Proclamation took effect. The decree, issued by President Lincoln, freed the slaves in the areas "in rebellion against the United States." But blacks were still not recognized as equals by law and were not allowed to serve in the U.S. Army. Frederick Douglass, an outspoken former slave, was one of the **abolitionists** who urged the government to allow blacks to enlist. "Once you [let a black soldier] get an eagle on his button, and a musket on his shoulder and bullets in his pocket," said Douglass, "there is no power on Earth that can deny that he has earned the right to citizenship."

Lincoln was concerned that if the Union army broke this color barrier, some border states, such as slave-holding Maryland, would join the Confederacy. But after wrestling with the idea, the Union's leadership began to recruit black soldiers.

"Wherever our army has been there remain no slaves."
—*Robert Gould Shaw*

Robert Gould Shaw

Date of Birth:	October 10, 1837
Hometown:	Boston, Massachusetts
Loyalties:	Union
Rank:	Colonel
Heroic Moment:	Fort Wagner, South Carolina (July 18, 1863)

Recruits for the 54th came from throughout Massachusetts and outside the state.

Fort Wagner

Shaw was placed in charge of the new recruits, which included two of Douglass's sons. On July 18, 1863, the 54th led the attack on the Confederacy's heavily fortified Fort Wagner in South Carolina. The fort protected the entrance to Charleston Harbor. If the Federals captured the fort, they had a chance to capture Charleston.

Shoulder to Shoulder

As the sun set, Shaw rallied his men on the beach. Standing shoulder to shoulder, the 54th began its march. With bombs bursting and bullets whizzing by, the 54th surged over the sand dunes and wooden stakes that protected the fort.

The firing was hot and heavy. Shaw bravely led his men. He waved his sword and shouted, "Forward, 54th!" Shaw was quickly killed by enemy fire, and the attack failed. However, he and the 54th proved that there was no color barrier to bravery. The Confederates buried Shaw in a mass grave with his men.

The soldiers of the 54th were trained at Camp Meigs in Readville, just outside Boston.

Ulysses S. Grant

Ulysses S. Grant wasn't a good student at West Point. He preferred to read novels, rather than study. In school, Grant wore rumpled clothes and was shy and quiet. Yet he rose to become the most important general of the war.

Though the North and South fought bitterly, Ulysses S. Grant made certain that the conditions of surrender protected Southern soldiers from being tried for treason.

"Although a soldier by profession, I have never felt any sort of fondness for war, and I have never advocated it, except as a means of peace." —*Ulysses S. Grant*

Grant Takes Command

In Grant, Abraham Lincoln finally found a general who could defeat Robert E. Lee. Grant had won many battles in the west, including the Confederate stronghold of Vicksburg. In 1864, Lincoln put Grant in charge of all Union armies. Grant developed a plan to weaken the Confederacy. As he and the Army of the Potomac battled Lee, Union General William T. Sherman invaded Georgia.

Ulysses S. Grant

Date of Birth:	April 27, 1822
Hometown:	Point Pleasant, Ohio
Loyalties:	Union
Rank:	Lieutenant General, Commander of the Union Army
Heroic Moment:	Overland Campaign (1864–1865)

Pursuing Lee

In May 1864, Grant met Lee for a two-day fight in the Wilderness, the same tangle of woods where Lee had trapped Hooker during the Battle of Chancellorsville. Grant had Lee outnumbered, so Lee decided to turn the battle into a killing field. Lee hoped that a staggering loss of life would turn public opinion in the North against the war and cause Lincoln to lose his reelection.

The Wilderness, Again

The first day of battle on May 5 was chaos. Lee waited for Grant in the Wilderness. As the fighting raged, units on both sides were confused. Soldiers fighting for the same side accidentally killed one another. On May 6, the Union finally smashed through the center of the Confederate line. Brushfires raged across the Wilderness, burning hundreds.

"Butcher" Grant

Neither side won the battle. Any other Union general might have withdrawn to Washington. Not Grant. Although bloodied, Grant pursued Lee southward. For the next six weeks, Grant chased Lee across Virginia in the Overland Campaign. Each battle was horrific. Union casualties were so high that even some Northern newspapers called Grant a "butcher." But Grant's relentless pursuit forced Lee finally to surrender at Appomattox Court House, Virginia, on April 9, 1865.

Many artists of the time tried to render the moment when Ulysses S. Grant and Robert E. Lee met before signing the papers of surrender.

Before the Overland Campaign, Union forces attempted to capture Richmond. During the Overland Campaign, the new objective was to destroy Lee's army.

William T. Sherman

> "Every attempt to make war safe will result in humiliation and disaster." —*William T. Sherman*

William Tecumseh Sherman considered himself a failure. "I am doomed to be a vagabond," he said. Yet Sherman was one of the war's greatest heroes, admired in the North and hated in the South.

Cruel and Swift

Sherman fought alongside Ulysses S. Grant in the west, then was ordered to lay waste to Georgia. Sherman and his troops marched into Atlanta in September 1864. They captured and destroyed the city. This assured the reelection of President Abraham Lincoln. It also crushed Southern morale. "War is cruelty, and you cannot refine it," Sherman said. "The crueler it is, the sooner it will be over."

Sherman's Goal

After burning Atlanta, Sherman boldly cut himself off from supply lines and marched to the Atlantic coast. He split in half his army of 98,000 troops, spreading his forces over a 60-mile front. His men lived off the land during the 250-mile march. Sherman's goal was to destroy the South's will to fight. "The utter destruction of [Georgia's] roads, houses, and people," Sherman wrote, "will cripple their military resources… I can make Georgia howl!"

William T. Sherman

Date of Birth:	February 8, 1820
Hometown:	Lancaster, Ohio
Loyalties:	Union
Rank:	Major General
Heroic Moment:	March through Georgia (1864–1865)

As an important center for the railways and commerce, Atlanta was a Union target.

To the Sea

Sherman's soldiers destroyed factories, military targets, and plantations. They destroyed railroads by prying up the lines and twisting them around trees. Some troops looted gold, silver, and other treasures.

Savannah, Georgia, was Sherman's goal. The Union navy had blockaded the South, but smugglers often broke the blockade to bring badly needed supplies to the Confederates. Savannah was a smuggler's paradise. Sherman captured Savannah on December 21, 1864. He then turned north to the Carolinas. Together with Grant, who was chasing Lee through Virginia, Sherman helped destroy the Confederacy.

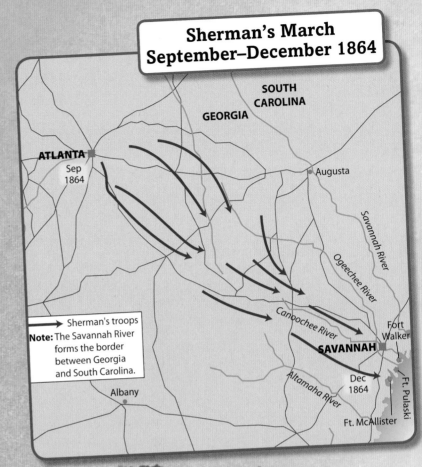

Sherman's March September–December 1864

SOUTH CAROLINA

GEORGIA

ATLANTA
Sep 1864

Augusta

Savannah River

Ogeechee River

Canoochee River

Fort Walker

→ Sherman's troops
Note: The Savannah River forms the border between Georgia and South Carolina.

SAVANNAH

Dec 1864

Altamaha River

Ft. Pulaski

Albany

Ft. McAllister

Brother vs. Brother

Many other battle leaders played key roles in the Civil War. Here are some of their stories.

Philip H. Sheridan (Union)

In 1864, Major General Philip H. Sheridan led a campaign in the Shenandoah Valley that helped the Union win the war. General Grant ordered Sheridan and his cavalry to follow Confederate General Jubal Early "to the death." By March 1865, Sheridan was victorious.

Before the Civil War, Philip H. Sheridan mainly served at U.S. posts in the frontier.

Lifelong sailor David G. Farragut served as a youth in the War of 1812.

David G. Farragut (Union)

In 1862, David G. Farragut led a **flotilla** of Union warships that captured the strategic port of New Orleans and blocked the Mississippi. He is even more famous for capturing Mobile, Alabama, in 1864. Mobile was the last Confederate port on the Gulf of Mexico.

George G. Meade (Union)

General George G. Meade took command of the Army of the Potomac three days before the Battle of Gettysburg. He is remembered for his heroic defense on Cemetery Ridge on the last day at Gettysburg. Later, he helped Grant defeat Lee during the Overland Campaign.

George G. Meade moved from Spain to the United States when his father died. Meade entered the military academy for financial reasons.

Jubal A. Early (Confederacy)

Jubal A. Early was so outspoken that Robert E. Lee called him his "bad old man." Early fought in many of the war's major battles. His most spectacular performance was at Manassas. He led a late-afternoon charge on July 21, 1861, that forced the Union soldiers to flee back to Washington.

Jubal A. Early served the Southern army despite voting against secession.

Lewis A. Armistead (Confederacy)

Lewis A. Armistead had dropped out of West Point, but was highly respected by his soldiers during the war. At Gettysburg, Armistead marched at the head of his brigade with his hat on his sword's tip so his men would not lose sight of him. He was killed just as he reached the Union lines.

Lewis A. Armistead was nearly kicked out of West Point after breaking a dish on Jubal A. Early's head.

George E. Pickett (Confederacy)

George E. Pickett led Pickett's Charge against the Union line at Cemetery Ridge on the final day at Gettysburg. Ironically, he had little to do with its planning though it now bears his name. During the charge, 13,000 Confederates bravely advanced into Union cannon fire. The Rebels suffered 6,000 casualties.

George E. Pickett surrendered with 800 of his men at Appomattox Court House.

Women of War

Men weren't the only heroes of the Civil War. Women played important roles, too.

Clara Barton

Clara Barton was a government employee at the U.S. Patent Office in Washington, D.C., when the Civil War began. While in Washington, she collected food and medical supplies for Union troops. The government then gave her permission to travel to the battlefields, where she worked as a nurse and helped distribute supplies. After the war, Barton helped families locate missing soldiers. She later organized the American Red Cross.

Clara Barton became known as the "Angel of the Battlefield."

Harriet Beecher Stowe

Upon meeting Harriet Beecher Stowe in 1862, President Lincoln remarked, "So this is the little lady who made this big war." Born in Litchfield, Connecticut, in 1811, Stowe wrote *Uncle Tom's Cabin*, one of the most important books of its time. The novel highlighted the cruelties of slavery. Stowe gained insight about slave life by interviewing former slaves and visiting a Southern plantation. Published in installments in 1851 and 1852, the novel fortified the anti-slavery movement in the North.

Harriet Beecher Stowe won a writing award at age 12 for an essay called "Can the Immortality of the Soul be Proved by the Light of Nature?"

Belle Boyd

While some women dressed as men in order to fight in the Civil War, Belle Boyd took a different approach. She became one of the South's most famous spies, beginning her cloak-and-dagger life when she was just 17. Legend has it she became a spy after Union soldiers ripped a Confederate flag from outside her home, replaced it with a Union banner, and then insulted her mother. Boyd was so angry that she shot one of the soldiers. Union officials later cleared her of any crime. During her career as a spy, Boyd eavesdropped on the conversations of Union officers and rode on horseback at night carrying secret messages.

Belle Boyd was imprisoned for spying in 1862 and was released in 1863 for health reasons.

Rose O'Neal Greenhow

Rose O'Neal Greenhow was a fashionable woman of Washington society. She was also a Rebel spy. She once sent a secret message to Confederate General Pierre Beauregard that helped him win the first battle of Manassas in 1861. Union officials imprisoned Greenhow. Yet she was still able to send secret messages to Confederate leaders. Finally, Union officials sent Greenhow back to the Confederacy. She later toured Europe, talking about the Confederate cause.

Rose O'Neal Greenhow (right) used a secret code to send messages.

Up from Slavery

During the war, thousands of Southern slaves attempted to flee to freedom in the North. Many heroic slaves and former slaves led their people to safety. Many pushed the abolitionist fight.

Harriet Tubman

In 1849, Harriet Tubman escaped from the slave state of Maryland. Yet she repeatedly risked her life by returning to the South as a "conductor" of the Underground Railroad. The Underground Railroad was a secret organization that helped slaves escape from the South. People who guided escaping slaves were known as conductors. For 10 years, Tubman secretly led hundreds of escaping slaves north to freedom.

As a young girl, Harriet Tubman's master beat her so much, she wore multiple layers of clothing for protection.

Frederick Douglass

Frederick Douglass was one of the nation's most important abolitionist leaders. He pressed President Lincoln not only to free the slaves, but also to allow blacks to serve in the Union military. Douglass had been born into slavery near the town of Easton, Maryland, in 1818. He learned to read and write, which was against the law. In 1838, Douglass escaped. He made his way to Massachusetts, where he worked repairing ships. At a meeting of the Massachusetts Slavery Society, he delivered a moving speech about the horrors of slavery. He soon became the chief African-American spokesperson against slavery.

Frederick Douglass escaped from slavery by dressing as a sailor and borrowing identification papers from a seaman.

Sojourner Truth

Sojourner Truth was born a slave in Ulster County, New York, in 1797. At the time she went by the name Isabella Baumfree. Because slaves were considered property, Isabella's white masters sold her several times. In 1827, New York abolished slavery. Isabella moved to New York City and began working as a servant.

In 1843, Baumfree changed her named to Sojourner Truth. She published her autobiography and toured the country making speeches against slavery. In 1864, Sojourner Truth moved to Washington, D.C., and fought against a city policy of not allowing blacks to sit on trains with whites. President Lincoln was so impressed with the courageous former slave that he invited her to the White House. She died in 1883.

Sojourner Truth spoke Dutch until age 9, when she was sold to an English-speaking family.

Glossary

abolitionists—people in favor of abolishing slavery

arsenal—a store or collection of weapons

bayonets—pointed blades that fit on the end of a rifle

brigade—a military unit made up of one or more units of infantry

cavalry—soldiers on horses

compromise—the middle ground in a dispute

Congressional Medal of Honor—the highest U.S. military honor a soldier can receive

counterattacked—an attack made in response to an enemy's attack

flank—the extreme right or left side of an army

flotilla—a small fleet of ships

objective—the goal of a military move or maneuver

outflank—to move around the extreme right or left side of an army

pontoon—a floating structure that can serve as a temporary bridge

reinforcements—additional people and equipment sent into a military operation

seceded—to have broken away from

tactician—a person who plans an action or a maneuver for combat

territories—regions in the U.S. that had their own governments but were not yet part of any state

Index